Growing up Safe

Safety
at the playground

Illustrated by Sue Wilkinson

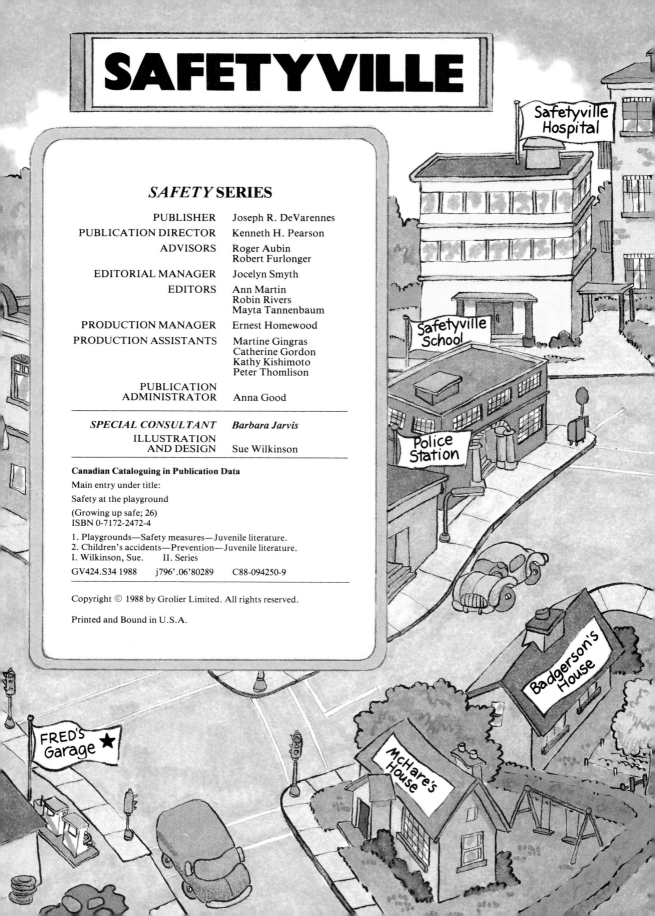

SAFETYVILLE

SAFETY SERIES

PUBLISHER	Joseph R. DeVarennes
PUBLICATION DIRECTOR	Kenneth H. Pearson
ADVISORS	Roger Aubin
	Robert Furlonger
EDITORIAL MANAGER	Jocelyn Smyth
EDITORS	Ann Martin
	Robin Rivers
	Mayta Tannenbaum
PRODUCTION MANAGER	Ernest Homewood
PRODUCTION ASSISTANTS	Martine Gingras
	Catherine Gordon
	Kathy Kishimoto
	Peter Thomlison
PUBLICATION ADMINISTRATOR	Anna Good

SPECIAL CONSULTANT	*Barbara Jarvis*
ILLUSTRATION AND DESIGN	Sue Wilkinson

Canadian Cataloguing in Publication Data

Main entry under title:

Safety at the playground

(Growing up safe; 26)
ISBN 0-7172-2472-4

1. Playgrounds—Safety measures—Juvenile literature.
2. Children's accidents—Prevention—Juvenile literature.
I. Wilkinson, Sue.   II. Series

GV424.S34 1988   j796'.06'80289   C88-094250-9

Come join Kim, Timmy and Tina Badgerson as they find out everything they need to know about playground safety.

ALWAYS GO TO THE PLAYGROUND WITH A GROWNUP.

WEAR SHOES IN THE PLAYGROUND.

TAKE TURNS ON PLAYGROUND EQUIPMENT.

DO NOT PUSH OTHERS ON THE SLIDE OR ON ANY OTHER PLAYGROUND EQUIPMENT.

ONLY ONE PERSON SHOULD GO DOWN THE SLIDE AT A TIME.

WAIT UNTIL THE SWING HAS STOPPED BEFORE GETTING OFF.

SIT, DO NOT STAND, ON SWINGS.

STAY WELL BACK FROM MOVING SWINGS. YOU CAN'T BE SURE THEY WON'T HIT YOU.

A GROWNUP CAN HELP YOU GET OFF A TEETERTOTTER SAFELY.

DO NOT THROW SAND. IT COULD GET IN SOMEONE'S EYES.

NEVER PUSH SOMEONE WHO IS DRINKING FROM A FOUNTAIN.

DO NOT RUN NEAR THE EDGE OF THE WADING POOL.

IF YOUR TOY GOES OUTSIDE THE PLAYGROUND, ASK A GROWNUP TO GET IT FOR YOU.